I Forgive Me…

I Am Free

I forgive me…I am free, because I encompass the guts to say I allowed everything in my life! Following the world herd is now gone like yesterday's dawn as I am instantly free…

Robert Wilson

Editing by Amy Lignor

ISBN: 1938634071
ISBN-13: 978-1-938634-07-9

I Forgive Me… I Am Free

Cowboy Wisdom NLI Coaching

Undauntedly unleashing my **Heart Visions** lifting the restrictions on 'Me' and my 'Posse of 3' to realize that **I Am The Quarterback in My Game of Life**. To unbridle my Daredevil Visionary and to 'Wow' the World, I understand and I soar in my Spiritual Zeal, opening the way for people to play in the Stalwart Autonomy of "I Forgive Me…I Am Free" to say: "I Abound in Bold & Astound Wisdom," allowing me to see I won my Game of Life because I choose to see I am a free lancing, dancing, dauntless avant-garde who is living life to the fullest every day to beam the gleam of love …

Thank you for purchasing, *I Forgive Me…I Am Free*

May_____

life flow in the lavish avalanche of
copious copiousness, now to eternity, in
the right way, in a loving way, under
grace in a Divine blessed way, and in
Divine order...**NOW!**

I FORGIVE ME... I AM FREE
By Robert A. Wilson

For more books like this one, visit Robert A. Wilson's website at:
http://cowboy-wisdom.com/

2013 copyright by Freedom of Speech Publishing, Inc.

Printed in the United States of America
The publisher offers discounts on this book when ordered in bulk quantities. For more information, contact Sales Department, Phone 815-290-9605, Email:
sales@FreedomOfSpeechPublishing.com

Product and company names mentioned herein are the trademarks or registered trademarks of their respective owners.

Freedom of Speech Publishing, Leawood KS, 66224
www.FreedomOfSpeechPublishing.com
ISBN: 1938634071
ISBN-13: 978-1-938634-07-9

A SPECIAL THANK YOU TO YOU!

On behalf of everyone at Freedom Of Speech Publishing, thank you for choosing I Forgive Me... I Am Free for your reading enjoyment.

As an added bonus and special thank you, for purchasing I Forgive Me... I Am Free, you can enjoy discounts and special promotions on other Freedom of Speech Publishing products. Visit www.freedomeofspeech.com/vip to learn more.

We are committed to providing you with the highest level of customer satisfaction possible. If for any reason you have questions or comments, we are delighted to hear from you. Email us at cs@freedomofspeechpublishing.com or visit our website at: http://freedomofspeechpublishing.com/contact-us-2/.

If you enjoyed I Forgive Me... I Am Free, visit www.freedomofspeechpublishing.com for a list of similar books or upcoming books.

Again, thank you for your patronage. We look forward to providing you more entertainment in the future.

Acknowledgements

A heartfelt thanks to my Mom and Dad who have passed for being my parents and the work ethic and moral values they instilled in me. I understand I wasn't always the easiest child…

I thank my family and extended family: Nieces, Nephews, Aunts, Uncles, Cousins, Sisters and Brothers for being a part of my life.

I thank every one of my friends for being a part of my life.

I thank Amy Lignor (www.thewritecompanion.com): published author, editor, ghostwriter, reviewer, and a truly dynamic writer.

I thank God, Mrs. Universe, the womb of unconditional love and enterprising energies, all people, spiritual ethers, metaphysical realms, physical playgrounds, mystical magical heavens of miracles, and all realized and unrealized sources in the cosmos, for opening the way to authorize and allow me to experience my life, *my way*.

I thank all my listeners and guests on *Cowboy Wisdom NLI Radio* at:
www.blogtalkradio.com/cwbywsdm.

I am thankful for Patrick Kungle and Girard Sagmiller with *Freedom of Speech Publishing* for all they do for me.

I thank everybody who buys and reads in order to expand their lives in a perfect way.

I am thankful for my life everyday and in every way, under grace in a perfect way.

I love life and life loves me!

Contents

Robert A. Wilson

Preface

This vision is written in first person, so when you read this read it as if you, yourself, wrote it.

This vision opens the way for me to be free of drama with a simple forgiveness. How do I dramatize forgiveness and all personal expansion?

Reading out loud allows you to get off the 'practice field' into you game of plush prosperity.

I choose to let go and exit the 'practice field,' real-eye-zing that my game of life is played right before my very eyes. Every second of every day dawns my newborn sassy shrewdness…

I open my heart to ride my mountains of success which allows this vision to vitalize my vividness in experiencing my sired desires.

As I read this vibrant vision, I pronounce that: I energize my farsighted frontiersman to see my life with effrontery, and as an explorer I get up and go. So I open my trailblazing eyes to ride my ranges of wealth and success.

As I witness this **Cowboy Wisdom NLI Coaching** *Vibrant Vision*, I choose to electrify my inner prowess with a 'WOW'ing essence of energized emotional acumen.

As I choose to peruse this **Cowboy Wisdom NLI Coaching** *Vibrant Vision*, I choose to open your inner prowess, which authorizes me to eavesdrop on new worldly wisdom, visualize my chosen results, as I relish tasting my moneyed-up milk chocolate success I smell the roses of nirvana.

I listen to my inner acumen and feel the words energize my inquisitive entrepreneur...

This authorizes my wealthy inner success to explode as I relish experiencing these visionary words to expand my inner landscape, broadening...

My rainbow brilliance from within, which embellishes my core décor to soar unsheathing my imaginative intuition...

I Forgive Me…I Am Free

I forgive me…I am free, because I encompass the guts to say I allowed everything in my life! Following the world herd is now gone like yesterday's dawn as I am instantly free…

Because I forgive me, which unleashes my dauntless decree to see me sailing away emotionally emancipated as I real-eyes that I am wise and in harmony with heart supremacy…

When I say, I forgive me…I am free, because I encompass the braveries to say I was shy – unwilling to listen to my inner peerless seer opens my epiphany eyes to realize I was living down…

…Down to society's sliding scale of hypocrisy. So I now recognize I allowed everything in my life, trying to fit into society's school system, comparing crap one to another underlying communal conceit…

Telecasting the snobby, medicated mundane which invoked sprained brain and ingrained patterns of "listen to me!" It's all about me! This unshackles me…

In all facets of my life to fly audaciously, canonizing enterprising tenacity saying all my guilt and indignity…

In my life is done and spun into oblivion; this authorizes me to let go and expand out of blaming me for anything that occurred in my life which instantly unblocks this parvenu eulogy...

I realize blame is being lousy at managing everything every day, sending me down the slide of shame that is bathed in silly, hapless, antagonizing memories. THIS ENDS NOW!

Because I listened to other people's agenda instantly goes up in flames, sanctions me to say blame and shame glided away in a perfect way and slithered into obscurity instantly to infinity...

Because other people tried to place their immaturity and insecurity upon me which opened my warrior eyes to see it was their cross to carry...NOT MINE!

So now I say "thank you" for my newborn wisdom and canonized courage; I encompass every situation that now sets me free to say "thank you" to that situation or person as I say goodbye.

This sanctions me to fly from my ingrained selfish pain to expand into understanding. I am exhibiting heart heroism as I unfetter my senses to experience life in the present moment...

I avow my "WOW!" unrestricting my wise, owlish, wizard to win internally – zinging audacious, rebellious determination to live in my Promised Land of Prosperity, now to eternity...

In a pristine serene way and in a daring new Divine order within me as I now real-eyes I allowed society's victimizing ways to be my way of looking at situations in my life, indoctrinating...

Their snobbish silliness in my consciousness because I encompassed a follower's way of life as I let go of involving anybody in my ingrained patterns because my ego wants to involve others...

My heart desires me to be accountable for everything I allowed, so I send the ego for a long walk on a short pier, dunking it into the ocean of extinction, expanding out...

Of the drama and trauma of my ego unlatches the latch of attachment of me, including somebody else, was a flaw clawing at me and limiting my personal expansion...

As I unleash my kapish to see forgiveness, all is simplified when I say "thank you" to all involved for the heart energizing enlightenment...

Because I look at every situation real-'eyes'-zing I encompass the courage to experience the situation; to see that I stand tall afterward moves me forward and unbinds this fine new wisdom...

When I listened to other people's quackery I became subdued in their mouthy, gooey stew which is their way of belittling me because people fear saying:

"WOW! Look at _____ (*your name*)! _____ is free..."

Because I stood in the face of the adversity I came out standing tall, so now I let go of what other people say because they are massaging the chicken shy-sting ego...

As asinine, malevolent, conceited people belittle my confidence they shake my hand, slapping me on the back while stabbing me as well...

With their frothing at the mouth rabid fears running amuck in their inner landscape, they now realize they are unsure and afraid of their life's jubilee...

As they walked in a clouded conceit, swirling in the selfish turmoil, confirming the fact that they like to think they are smarter than the other person so they can go to bed every night in fearing frightened people...

May discover they are all they think they are. Thus, they live in a priggish prison within. So I go my way in a glow-grinning, luminous, omnificent "WOW!"...

As they go, I say "thank you" for the awesome new acumen as I unleash luminary luminosity in silence. I peruse my internal universe in pure clear visionary prowess...

As I open my effrontery eyes to realize silence speaks – internal love energizes – nirvana is canonized emotional ecstasy that excites my exhilarating, clairvoyant sapience; tantalizing audacious...

Superstar Yahweh to say: "Hey! I forgave me!" So I set the world free as I sashay through my day, free of competition by unleashing that harness and setting my eavesdropping entrepreneur free...

As I choose to expand in wisdom while the other one walks away talking indignant to themselves in a controlled condensation as I offer a frolicking smile externally and internally...

To speak a dawning new decree that I am a daring energy, canonizing revolutionary emotional emancipation in every facet and cell of my spiritual supremacy...

To jazz a jovial animated zeal, zooming into my savory daily extravaganzas...I am the mystical maestro of my omnific orchestra, authoring my trumpets to announce my arrival...

My drums beat forthright feats as my gleaming genius shines in the worldly vista, broadcasting my visionary intrepidness, speaking tenacious acuity...

Singing the praise of "I" – "I" am here today to say "thank you" to everybody for being a part of my journey through the jungles of the terra incognita...

As I have magically used the machete to force my way through my inner jungle to declare emotional revolutionary freedom in my soul, speaking omnipotent utopian lucidity, releasing the tether on my euphoric sagacity...

Opening my eyes to seeing that I was trying to control and manipulate the situation left me crying with a broken ego because I have never ever experienced a broken heart...

Because my heart is wise that when I listen to my heart smartness I sail around the world exuding a profound aura – awesome undaunted realizations and ardently seeing people...

As wisdom in motion opens me to win internally; speaking discerning, omnificent, moneyed-up outcomes as I fly on my charmed red carpet seeing the world in colorful charismatic character...

Unlocks the blocks to say "I forgive me...I am free" to see that every person is on their personal journey allows me to sunbathe in my beaches of billion-dollar bills...

In serene serenity...in the right way, in a loving way, under grace in a divine blessed way, and in Divine order instantly to infinity...NOW!

Beam the Gleam of Love

I beam the gleam of love when I am in the shimmering glimmer of letting go. This unlatches the locks and frees the attachments of my big-old-ego's muddling, befuddling stranglehold of inner scenery...

The woe of the medication of the societal education that is my self-imposed limitation ingrains the pain of what other people think is the "stink of my think," exposing cloning...

Of my knowing; hoodwinking of my over thinking; smearing of the fears of change as the caustic cause of my couch-potato-I-tice creating...

My apathetic apparatus by transforming my lackadaisical self peels scarring scabs of heal, and opens the wounds of my victimizing. Why is this happening?

...To my plastering the past in the forefront of my conscious mind that love is blind opens the way for me to see past the fact that this is all a plaster cast as sustained sprained brainwashing mobilizing immaturity...

Of insecurity, as the fairytale is uncovered to be the hideous smell that the material world sells; it is the enemy in the enema of would-da should-da could-da...

That creates the prattle and the rattle of my inner chatter which instills the illusionary pills of the insane, of the same dimes rhyme in subliminal mind to be the student...

Of the insane of the same opens the door for me to soar, unbridling my 'maharishi mastermind' to understand that I encompass superstar, audacious, natural discernment...

To unleash the kapish of celebrated, liberated, quick-witted, intrepid emotional sassiness which vitaliz-eyes-zes my free-flowing, forthright feelings to expand...

My innovative dynamisms; to electrify my bright light of my free-flowing, Divine white light by brightening my rainbow which lights my heart's delight by galvanizing...

My gallivanting, newborn, keen, pristine percipience, darting my heart's 'smarts' into the universal vista by adamantly articulating my love as lionized optimism vivaciously energizing and emblazing...

My lively oracle VIP eminence; walking the talk of my daring, new-fangled leadership by orchestrating virtuous endeavors; unshackling a long-awaited...

Life-force that is an ordained vista, enriching the milk chocolate landscape of the universe by unfastening lavish opulence, vivaciously...

Experiencing love, innovation, freedom and the enjoyment of a utopian cornucopia, living opulently...

Virtually expressing keen, pristine, laudable, optimistic verve and exulting in awesome, liberating, omniscient vim & vigor by embracing...

Who I am in my innermost prosperous prowess; this allows the yacht to leave the dock, launching my omnipotent visionary, empowering...

Luminary, owlish, vibrant, empery by unfettering the fame in brain and unhinging my singing, fervent, astute monarch and entertaining my leisure; opalescent valorous effervescence...

To serenely sunbathe on my beaches of plush prosperity to loll-n-stroll to a very effusive, never-ending, cascading cash flow to relish the flow of my awe-inspiring "live and let live"...

Originality; vacationing everyday in an extraordinary way in the "glow of my go," to love openly, victoriously, every day in the present moment – in every way, in the right way; in a loyal way under grace, in a picture perfect way to wine and dine myself in the primetime of my Divine Order – in the "POW" of the "WOW" of NOW!

Stalwart Autonomy

I gallantly gallop in stalwart autonomy to wallop the world with winning wisdom, as I unleash omnipotent gumption, ascending laudable, lionhearted, omniscient prowess...

To broaden my nobility...I am a mobile monarch opening bona-fide interstellar luster; enthralling prodigious prodigies in people's visionary seascape authorizes me...

To see every day as surplus cash appears promptly, energizing enterprising endeavors that forever expand my luxurious lifestyle...

This Unleashes my flashy wisdom wallop and unclutters worldwide codswallop as I unfurl my whirlwinds of swirling, sumptuous wealth in my worldly opportunities, alluring me...

To mesmerize my visualization by accenting my global adventurous luminary liveliness optimizes preeminent judiciousness; this climaxes me into a calm, cool chillaxing state of mind...

Unrestricting my effortless effrontery eminence to radiate real charismatic audacious daredevil innovation; I tantalize the earth's ethers with soothsayer lore to be definitely sure...

I endure the race to realize awesome character energizes my moral and ethical values to vision affluence lionizing undaunted enterprising spirituality...

In my inner scenery; setting free a vehement vitality vibrating imaginative talisman acuity; lighting up inventive terrificness by "Yes-sing!"...

Every facet of my life to recognize that I am fantastic; expressing the sure-fired desire to walk the high wire of success because I discovered my euphoric heroic explorer in my cored décor...

To understand that nuggets of wisdom flow to me when I listen to hear the cosmic seer unlocking glowing genius and letting fly the omnificent, whimsical, intrinsic newborn with gallivanting gusto...

Unbridles my bodacious saddle-bronco rider valor to glide, generating my prodigious potentate gait to enjoy a date with innate straightforwardness unrestricting my royal, astute, robust...

Trust in my revered rebel to bust out in a rant and rave as I exterminate, "I can't," from the heart's and soul's of spirits that live in the DNA cells – the minds of people and the universal skies into un-constricting...

Canonized adroitness, naturalizing thunderous thrills, 'whooshes' a free rein to my high-spirited, purity which purifies my pioneering spirit setting free my undaunted, revolutionary, intrepidness...

Electrifying sapience to understand that I expand my, "I won my game of life in my heart!" because I dared with my dreamy, audacious, rabble-rousing tenacity unwinding a vim and vigor...

To win in my Divine skin, astonishing the world with new-fangled 'Mama Grizzly-Bear' awareness, mirroring Fred Astaire showcasing the elegance of Ginger Rogers on his arm, releasing a...

two-step ardor adeptness that unleashes my perky, articulate me and illuminates my pert eagerness to amazingly realize my triumphant campaigner, which ignites collaborating unity...

In letting go, ascending charismatic Yahweh opens the way for me to ride the mountain trails of panorama prosperity to lie so gallantly spry...

Basking in the sun on my beaches of bountiful bliss throughout the universe; cruising in a carefree spree – today and every day – in an effervescent way...

In a regal way, in a divine blessed heart, loving under grace in a glamorous, glorious way and in a crystal clear Divine order…NOW!

Because

How does the word "because" empower my eyes to focus?

The 'buzz' of "because" energizes a subtle, but direct path, for my inner landscape to facilitate.

Just sit quietly and say, "I am successful because..." My internal scenery becomes instantly engaged in my intentions, opening out my adventurous curiosity to visualize my desired outcome.

"Because," buzzes my subliminal landscape because it was always used in my childhood: Why did you do that? **Because!!!** Therefore, "because" is ingrained as a word of stainless significance to me...and everybody else.

When I say the word, "because," I energize my eyes and internal landscape in order to do things differently.

How do you respond to this affirmation? Instead of being in business or being a businesswoman/man because business tells your subconscious mind you are a busy-n-ess with 'ess' meaning person – all business tells you that you are a busy person. Business doesn't mean wealthy or successful. When I tell myself

I am busy and productive, I am soothing my ego and shutting off my enterprising innovator.

How do I feel when I say I am an enterprising innovator? What energizes me most? I am busy and productive. Or! I am an enterprising innovator.

Who am I trying to impress when I say I am busy and productive? What am I hiding from by telling people I am busy and productive? Busy and productive are nothing but silent fear that people try to impress other people with.

When I am the enterprising innovator I delegate and relegate tasks to competent people **because** I understand that I am competent and, in so doing, I realize I surround myself with competent people.

When I am enterprising my eyes and heart they are open and forward-focused. How do I feel in my inner scenery when I say this?

I unleash my enterprising innovator, freeing my entrepreneurial energies to be the facilitator of products that people love to buy and pay me effusively every day for. **Because** I listen relaxed and patient with myself; therefore, I am relaxed and patient with other people. I now understand when people are relaxed and feel at ease, they purchase my products in lavish avalanches; affluence becomes abundant today and every day. I expand and energize their lives in a rich way.

How do I feel when I say: "I am the facilitator of my business?" I feel a vibrant liberation in my heart. When I speak the words I open my eyes and authorize me to emancipate heart hierophant I become audaciously animated in my daily escapades

As I am looking for my opportunities...how do I look for opportunities in my daily encounters?

I never have a chance but I always am engulfed in the opportunity to expand my life, wealth, success and to enjoy my life my way. To verbalize this:

I can expand **because** I understand. I encompass a bold backbone unsheathing my zealous zeal and brilliantly electrifying my chutzpah, audible-eyes-zing undaunted sapience and edifying my dauntless dignity by broadening the facilitation of your products, expanding your brand, enhancing your cascading cash flow today and every day – in a picture perfect way.

Finish these "Buzz of Because" affirmations...

I am successful because...
I expand my brand because...
I canonize my cascading cash flow because...
I am good at what I do because...

I love myself because…
I am good in managing money because….
I am relaxed at business because…
I am patient with myself because…
I deserve all my divine wealth because…
I am deserving of a lavish, never-ending flow of clientele because…
I embrace my wisdom because…

Hence…the lesson is learned! NOW!

I Am The Quarterback of My Game of Life

I am the quarterback of my game of life, which opens my eyes to my quarterbacking talent and sanctions me to unleash my gun-slinging Hall of Fame Quarterback...

To throw deep into the end zone because Mrs. Universe, the womb of lavish avalanches of abundance, is my speedy wide receiver and hears my every sired desire...

Authorizes me to unmask my inner defensive mechanism, effortlessly emancipates my warrior quarterback and unbridles my brazen warrior to daringly untether...

My soothsayer synergy and turn loose my optimistic, quixotic, undaunted, audacious, rabble-rousing tenacity – energizing my revolutionary brilliance unravels my trendsetting quarterback...

Exhilarates my potentate innateness exposing my canonized, kinetic abilities as I gallantly grasp the fact that "God" is my offensive line; Infinite Spirit is my defensive line; my heart is my running back...

My gunfighter guts are my linebackers televising my titan knight boldness to stand tall behind my offensive line; God laudably liberates my Infinite Spirit to strip my chaotic opponents...

Of the football allowing Mrs. Universe, the womb of enterprising innovation and unconditional love, to be that speedy wide receiver as my canonized abilities are my speedy defensive backs...

My steadfast trust in my quarterback prowess is there as my fullback kicks the obstacles out of the way for my rebellious running back, as my engaging sage appears as the tight end, catching my enterprising passes with class.

My ever-expanding wisdom is my slot receiver as I now understand Infinite Spirit tackles...

My meddlesome melodrama with confident charisma, showcasing my colorful hegemony and authorizing the robust champion campaigner to ignite my quarterback...

Innovation magnetizing the atmosphere with a newborn genius that defense means Intuitive Spirit, as defense says...

"I daringly energize forward-looking enlightenment naturalizing enterprising fortunes" in my daily actions...

Because the offense knows where it is going, with the defense relying and applying their quickness and intuition...

To sniff out the rival offense's scheme as I now cognize that chaos is a schemer with zero self-esteem trying to steal my thunderous skill, as chaos is instantly drilled into the ground...

Since I unleashed my defensive frontline on my mischievous mundaneness with a frothing at the mouth stoutness because defense wins championships...

As my defense is filled with non-conformist campaigners sustaining my fearless foursome rebelliousness, I now appreciate my defense that showcases determination, effrontery, and feistiness...

Expanding newborn sapience, neutralizing offensive chaotic situations with speed, common sense and innate foresight, as my offense broadcasts forthright foresight, energizing ...

Natural superstar entrepreneurialism, exiting out of my inner defensive intensity that the world is against me – opens me out to understand I tackle the challenge with innovative foresight...

Allowing my linebackers to tackle the fringe fallacies, recovering that chaotic fumble, allowing my God to clear the way for my running back to run right at the challenge, unleashing…

My winning wisdom to beam a straight line to the goal line for the score, as my speedy wide receivers catch my cascading cash flow; as my tight end blocks for my running back…

Catching the flack and spiking the ball in face of the challenge – sending all my challenges to the 'showers' to flow down the drain, allowing me to free of mundane pain…

As I gain in stature, my steely sex appeal gleams gallant, luminary, excellence – aggrandizing magnificent stainless saintliness **because**, as the quarterback of my life…

I strive in chaos, thrive in challenge, and I arrive in my daily life feeling bountiful bliss realizing my game of life is won in the daily games I play with others…

Recognizing people are my wealth my engaging sagacious gutsiness is my success, as I now realize that I love my game of life…

Because I am in my 2-minute drill, frolicking in my piquant perkiness to see my dreams open up as I venture into my day – vibrant and alive to thrive with my visions in my mind's eye to see that…

I release and let go of something every day, opening the door for my rollicking riches to flow like a tight spiral through the air as I walk like Joe Montana, televising...

My Hall of Fame Quarterback flair; portraying the galvanizing gusto of legendary Dick Butkus; emanating the titan tenacity of the Steel Curtain in Pittsburgh...

The speed and agility of Gayle Sayers, running back, at the goal line leaving would-be tacklers with nothing but air to cling to; exuding the get up and go of Jack Youngblood...

Who played a game with a broken leg; running with gracefulness of Lynn Swann; catching a pass while falling down unfurls my fullback ferociousness of "Moose" Johnson, hampering my never-ending...

Itching of my bitching attitude, of Walter Peyton who is forever known as "Sweetness," who played his whole career with Da' Bears never exuding or saying: "It's all about me..."

Every day, both offensively and defensively, I play and lay my expanding emotional epiphanies in front of me as I unleash my linebacker, listening for my defensive back gazelle deftness...

To see where I am off-track, tackling the quaking quack of smack that talks tough when on the bluff runs in the face of a my inner fullback because the quaking quack understands…

My fullback tenacity will smack him and lay him flat on his back – for it is better to turn tail in fail and run away to another hill to spill its inner lies because, when a slacking…

Smacker enters my life they pass away as I hoist my super bowl trophy high in the air, basking in my game of success and patting myself on the back for understanding that I have won my game of wealth…

Because I gallantly displayed that I encompassed the wisdom-energizing affluence – loving today and harmonizing my endless cascading cash flow to lavishly stroll into my prosperity accounts…

Instantly…in the majestic, right way; in a laudable, lively, loving way' into my life from now to eternity in a rich, robust way; and in Divine order…NOW!

Dime the Rhyme

"Eye," emotionally feel the zooming zeal of my
Polar Bear moxie, unleashing my core kapish to
soar into the wild frontier of my terra incognita
by increasing my grit and get…

To grease the release of letting go; fitting into
the stink of society's "think fink of my think
hoodwink of corporate over think" medication
of the societal, mandated education…

That condones corporate fascism by cloning and
binding people's minds – spraining their brain
with ingrained brainwashing of political
correctness that fits into society's ills is the
pill…

That people swallow in order to wallow in the
hollow of society's silliness, overreacting,
controlling, insipid, enslaving tempest – yoking
of the senseless robber baron greed…

As 'powers to be' ride their pride in their slow
ride of slime and grime of low self-esteem
dictating their inner pain into a physical bland-
scape; to invoke a yoke of yuk upon…

The people by saying: "Look at me! I am the
pain ace ruining your day!" because they want
you to suffer as much as they are suffering in

their inner paradox that is filled with chicken pox...

So they itch their inside by inflicting their agonizing, egotistical arrogance that showcases their material baby-eyes-zed immaturity...

Because 'powers to be' smear their fears in the never-ending worthless stuff-n-fluff that people listen to and accept as the fake-n-bake news of the day...

Which is filled with fables of fallacy; allowing me to see the insane of the same opens the way for me to unlock my savant cleverness, authorizing my titanium backbone to rise and shine, giving...

A free reign to my Yahweh to open the way for me to see that I am flying high in the rigor of my vigor, to vividly, innovatively, generating opulence by realizing...

I am the real deal when I am glistening, listening, and optimizing wizardry to beam my keen pristine percipience animates my awesomeness...

As my sunlight of copious cornucopia brightens my heart's delight, enlightening my serene serenity of my inner prayer and revealing instant success; tantalizing...

Intuitive, new-fangled endeavors to party like an energized, radicalized conquistador; igniting prosperity, infusing nimble-witted courtliness, exhilarating me...

To hear the 'hoorah' of accomplishment to acclaim the fame of my talisman talent... This ignites my sagacious sage's internal flame to thrive in primetime...

To dime the rhyme of daring, innovative magnificence – every day in every way – in my super conscious mind; I am free to zing the ring of my own Liberty Bell...

Christening my 'Christ' within to sing in order to understand the crescent of the present frees me to cast the past as the present, to be the raging sage, unbridling...

My real astute genius and imagining newborn genuine stalwart acumen by galvanizing enterprising wit to walking in the moment to mirror my decree, amplifying...

My dignity; edifying my credence; revolution-eyes-zing expansive emancipation to feel the salt air of success on my face...

To feel the emerald grass between the toes of the mountains of wealth to see my universal cascading cash flow that fills my bank account so I walk on my mountain overlooking...

the oceans of love that I experience in every facet of my life – today and every day – to emotionally aggrandize my inner grand-eye-zed landscape; to experience me sitting on...

My front porch of my visionary villa rocking in the panorama of immaculate rainbow tranquility, in a rich milk chocolate way...NOW!

"Eye" See I Am Innovatively Alive;

Unleashing My Enterprising Drive

"Eye" see I am innovatively alive unleashes my enterprising drive to glide, enjoying the ride on the universal tide, obliging...

The world with my "get up and go" liveliness, igniting my dauntless...

Ennobling vitality to be my reality unchains my sustaining vim of my intra-national maharishi, unlocking...

My cosmic mahatma oracle brilliantly invigorates my lively emancipating eminence, magnetizes...

My visual, adventurous cosmos with my august aura unbinds my divining Diviner, unhampering my gallivanting scamper of my swashbuckling Divine enterpriser...

To see all my ports in the galaxy as phenomenal opportunity as I "paint the town red" to feel the acceleration of my exhilaration of my exoneration while, driving my Rolls Royce and voicing...

My robust enthusiasm to experience my life-expanding opportunities with gallant gutsiness, to compassionately say: "I exude frontrunner style which profiles my entertaining entrepreneur..."

Sauntering onto the stage at the Ryman Auditorium to play my Grand Old Opera songs: "I am Innovative Alive!" astounds the world stage by singing, "Enterprising Drive," telling the world that...

I arrived, strived, and thrived electrifies the universe; enlivened newborn Bugatti Veyron exquisite tenacity to say: "By God, I Bugatti all my sired desires," showing the world stage...

I was unafraid to engage my intra-hero brio to be the champion, placing my Hall of Fame star on my mantle because I encompassed the mettle...

To show the world I embodied the sassy 'pizzazz' to put the *varoom* in my Veyron as I exhibited my Bugatti Veyron moxie...

I am the sage with an innovative regal rage singing: "Take the Pessimism of the World and Shove It!" into the oven to be obliterated into ash, opening the way for my sashay onto the...

Stage to sing my songs of pristine prosperity in harmony with my sired desires ignites my Grand Ole' Opry opportunities...

That I partake in money endeavors as they eight skate and donate to my prosperity accounts in a gigantic way from all sources in the universe in an easy, effortless way...

As I realize when I participate in daily escapades with an undefended ear I hear my cascading opportunities, opening my eyes to feel me unseal my emotional lore to assure my peerless seer...

To unleash my debonair doctrinaire as my stout-hearted composure unsheathes my entrepreneurial composer, exposing my undaunted utopian songwriter...

Authorizes brighter, bolder songs to flow through my vocal cords, harmonizing my lips with savvy songs of success as I sip on the wines of wealth from vineyards, innovative ideas...

As I see my visualizations and initiate my nirvana persona, enamoring "YES"-ses admiring real, discerning sapience to be the vim and vigor...

Incites the excitement from my superstar visionary ardor, enlivens my lightning bolts of sapience to form my intra-zeal appeal...

Tantalizes my innovative ovulations naturally signifies my "Hell, Yeah!" from my inner "YEA"-sayer, expressing my prosperity prayers setting ablaze an amazing grace light in my dignified iron-will...

To write my electrify words and sing of my adventurous daredevil wit to realize **I** am the prize to recognize and reveal to my conscious mind...

My precise date with destiny that my desires will arrive with opulent pride because I choose to hop the **op**'s sailing...

To a new **por**t of lush prosperity to sing my **tun**es that fit the wit of my '**it**' saying "yes" **t**o my 'yea-sayer' **Y**ahweh...

OPPORTUNITY!

I yearn to discern to earn my cascading cash flow because I choose to unleash my "I can expand" understanding...

I encompass the sand, setting free my intrepid, canonized abilities naturally unsealing my enterprising-wise, opening my entrepreneurial eyes to see...

My life 'flows in the go' of galvanizing gusto because I choose to discern understanding, I can unseal my revolutionary ideals to be the real deal told me…

"Yes! I can be a Grand Ole' Opry singer" today and every day, standing on the trendsetter stage singing my 'Global Get Up and Go' understanding that I am **thee** (yes, THEE and not 'the') entertainer of the year…

To be my superior prophet singing prosper-eyes-zing pizzazz from my core décor to see my entrepreneurial albums debut in the day's-view at number one on my pay-per-view window…

Because I choose to endow the "WOW!" of my Divine destiny with predestined intestinal fortitude in songs that I sing amplifying affluence, so now I choose to pose for my prosperity picture…

As I sip tea on my veranda of Ponderosa, enjoying my bountiful bonanza and understanding I expanded the wisdom of the world because…

I chose to be innovative and alive, unleashing my enterprising drive today in an opulent, opportune way to bask in copious opulence in an innovative, enterprising way and in Divine order…NOW!

Heart Visions

"Eye" unlock my **heart wisdom vision**, opening out my utopian listening prowess to hear the magical revelations from my godly genius that invoke a 'Scooby Doo' moment…

In my mental imagery, making me go 'errrr' in my conscious countryside; however, my subliminal scenery says 'ahhh' exuding a forward looking curiosity…

Authorizing me to set sail on a snappy new avatar adventure NOW, because my omniscient kernel understands that my heart wisdom visions are forever and always flowing easily from…

My saintly savant who opens out the trails that lead from my deserted desert-poverty consciousness and victimizing poverty DNA encryptions…

Into the omnipotent oasis of sanguine wisdom – infinite innovation surfing on an ebb tide of ever-flowing love and animated laughter, encrypting my DNA with a plush prosperity cryptogram…

Freeing my inner landscape to feel, smell, taste, touch, hear – AND BELIVE – luscious luxury as the way I am experiencing life now and forever in every facet of my life...

As my sagacious sapience enriches the ethers of the universe, people feel free to grasp unlimited wealth and paramount success in a savvy sumptuous way...

As I easily, effortlessly, and continuously walk in the Divine light of copious utopia – today and every day – under grace, in a picture perfect way...NOW!

Daredevil Visionary

"Eye" see I am the **daredevil visionary** by understanding that my life mirrors snowboarding on an avalanche cascading down a mountain side…

Because perils of challenge are right under me and around me; however, when I energize my forthright focus on my adventurous journey down the mountain…

I swish and swirl, sending forth my angelic deftness, grizzly bear moxie, grit-n-get attitude, and my savant sapience, opening the way for my serene, moralizing life…

To flow in optimizing harmony with me experiencing my cherished outcomes, to relish my beloved journey and to bask in lavish avalanches of copious abundance…

As I "move-n-groove" with an open heart, letting my higher self and core wit be the mover and shaker of my daily life by listening to my untested intuitiveness and trusting my innovative ingenuity…

As a truss of white light gallantly galvanizes my avatar abilities that beam from my glorious godliness, I encompass to snowboard, like an Olympic Gold Medalist…

Through profound, enlivened, entertaining events in a preeminent prosperous way – electrifying the atmosphere with an "I can expand" attitude...

As I enjoy life's high voltage of success in a picture perfect way, I am sitting in the lodge drinking hot chocolate and enjoying the lush opulence in a Gold Medal way...NOW!

I Abound in Boldness & Astound With Wisdom

I abound in boldness and astound with wisdom mirroring endless beautiful bliss that I see in the sheen, pristine blue skies of my mind's eye, emulating...

The brazen, bold, beautiful brilliance of the Teton Mountains, photocopying me, looking across the posh plushness of 'Savannah's' of the world, visual-eyes-zing the pristine prosperity that mirrors...

The vast prairies of the West; to glide in the stride of my preeminent prominence, showcasing my stout-hearted resolve to revolutionize enterprising sagaciousness...

Optimizing lively visions, expanding the wisdom of understanding that I expand my "I can" attitude when I real-eyes my canonized abilities naturalize my success...

So when I choose to let go of saying "think" and "know," because when I say these words I am in the blizzard of the 'fink of my think; stuck in the stink of my over think' and wallowing...

In my 'know it all stall,' slithering in my arrogant crawl, spiraling down to my egotistical fall, landing me in the smell of my tell and eating my humble pie – translated as the "pooh" in my stew…

Binding my subconscious mind in my small pox paradoxes, creating my material immaturity of my disallow mindset which constipates my mind that has me living…

In the insane of the mundane; so now is the time for the fool in me to be flushed down the stool, unbinding my titanium spine to ride the money train into the promised land of…

Prosperity, realizing omnipotence by magnificently innovating success, enjoying the delicacies of life by loving infinite freedom and electrifying my spirit, mind, body…

To experience a bountiful bliss of my lively lithe; to relish my lavish luxurious life in a sassy, sexy, loving way…NOW!

Me and My Posse of 3

Me and posse of 3 pray for peace and prosperity as we ride my open range that is free of barbwire fences, liberated from boundaries branding my life's wealth and success that maverick's roust out…

My moneyed-up astute visionary energized innovation revolutionizes my canonized kinetic sapience and spurs my dauntless cowboy "get up and go"…

Ride the winds of the unknown; rope the tornados of triumph with a calf roping swiftness; hearing frontier breezes of a rancher's luminary lore sets free my posse of 3 and me to ride astride…

Our 17-hand steely gray studs to run thunderously across the mountain valleys, understanding we are lightning bolt fast when drawing out six shooters of illuminated insight…

In the face of the 'Chaos Kid' to sending the crooked-nosed villain to the Promised Land to never show his/her face again, showcases my mountain-bred heart, thoroughbred sleek speed range…

Horse wrangler 'wise,' listening as I gallop on my opportunity ranges engages my mountain man feistiness, frontier sharpness, titan tenacity, and unlocks my sharpshooter eyes on my prosperity prize...

As the range rolls along in idyllic quietness, this saturates my body and sanctions my noisy mind to settle down in philosophical awareness, opening my core idiosyncrasies to relax, relishing...

The pristine scenery, with my stealthy cavalryman ears pealed to my surroundings for an enterprising surprise, relying on my warrior wise that is 'dialed in' to the open prairie with mountains...

Standing tall and proud; with me stoutheartedly seeing the magnificent mural of my sired desires in the sky above the mountain tops covered with virgin snow, televising their gleaming gusto...

As I profoundly realize that prayer opens my silent visionary savvy, enticing peace, optimizing sensational silence, emblazing prosperity, sovereign-eye-zes sumptuous success, exhilarating...

My money-making magician intuition so I instantly see me witnessing the instant reveal of my $1,200,000 per month cash flow to glow from...

My overflowing, plush prosperity accounts, because I authorize and allow myself to understand that my life expands through prayer and peace…

Bountifully blooms today and every day, in every way, in plush prosperity to live in silence of emotional enterprising élans living in the space of my thoughts, seeing every opportunity…

In my visionary listening opens worldly trendsetting eyes, unleashing my spry debonair flair, artfully airing my posse of 3 spirited spree, sending me into newborn excitement…

In my farsighted frontiersman to have fun exploring the monetary magic of the universe with a perverse astuteness, realizing every person on this earth is my newborn stealth, wealthy wisdom…

As I am the District Attorney of my journey to query the new people and experiences on my quest, expanding my trailblazing willingness to understand life expands in listening and exalts…

My road-weary warrior soulful heartiness to confess I encompass the feisty farsightedness to realize my audacious willingness to trust…

My innate abilities to hear the seer inside my life experiences rather than fall into a trap of 'crap' that this happened because **I** was bad, now I am sad is flushed down the stool…

As I let go of being a sad fool by expanding into a soothsayer fool fostering omniscient omnificence, loving life in a titan thriving way. As I physically think I am tired in my egotistical mind…

I create my faltering adulterous apathy as a "pity me" searing fallacy for my haughty laziness as it squeals when my sassy spirit full of vim and vigor appears and is ready to run at the speed of light delights…

My hearted knight to ride into my mountainous terra incognita with my knight mounted on my stallion with lionized love for battle, mirroring my soul's steely foresight that unlocks…

My bold, billionaire flair to stare in my mirror unrestricting; this undoes the 'buzz' of my star-powered spirit to realize I am nuclear fission, introducing my emotional enterprising energy…

As uncontrollable entrepreneurial electricity, inciting my capitalistic turbines in my innovative power lines, delivering undoubted intuitive wisdom …

To extract my sovereign sagacity to expand my world traveler diversity; to feel at home in every situation, I discover I have landed – letting go of the bland bantering I have swirling around...

In my core conditioning because I recognize the wise in allowing people to speak in any tone they choose, opening my luminary listening to hear their frustration as positive proficiencies...

To realize their frustration spurs my frustration into newborn sapience, as their positive libretto assures my potentate prowess I heard neonatal wisdom flow into my ears...

I hear my forward-looking acumen stoutheartedly enter my astounding intrepid inventor 'go-getter' wit, inciting my inner landscape rings zestful peace to radiate from my savant soul...

To sing out loud, unsheathing laudable prayer, televising 'sunrise-wise' peace to illuminate my opulent opulence, beaming brilliant emancipated awesome magnificence, invigorating...

Nirvana grandeur; endearing my spirit, body and mind to realize my spirit entices me; my body is the range in which my happenstances occur to unfurl newborn innovation in my daily escapades...

With my 3 amigos – my heart, guts and wisdom – to rope the mavericks of money aggrandizing vivid emancipation in all my minds – revving-up innovative, keen-witted synergy...

Igniting a rainbow cash flow into my esteemed extravaganza I call life, shamelessly loving imaginative freedom, eulogizing my 'fun in the sun,' basking on my bountiful beaches...

I was challenged as I realized I encompass the guts to say
"I don't know." So, I let go. I let God expand through the challenge into galvanized gusto in every facet of my life...

Today and every day – in every way, in the right way, in a loving, blessed way under grace, in a loud, proud perfect way, and in a Divine order...NOW!

Triumphantly Terrific Tuesday

(Continue Reading Out Loud For the Best Outcome...)

As I read this vision I feel my heart become free and open; I allow the words to expand me and engage my heart to energize my conscious mind and visualize my sired desires.

I will allow myself to feel these words inflame my fame and fortune within, enabling me to see the 'flow of my galvanized gusto' – now to eternity – in sunlit, Divine order...

I am in a Triumphantly Terrific Tuesday, perusing my prudent student and unleashing my money-making monarch to march into my daily life with lively prophesying pluck, vehemently vitalizing...

My day-to-day dauntless astute Yahweh to open the way for me to play on my physical playground with astounding, profound patience to realize...

The world is full of individuals ardently asking for my streaming, intuitive, individualism – unleashing my imaginative spiritual magic to release their pessimism...

Unrestricting their entrepreneurial world with wise, omnificent revelations and allowing them to decree the universe is a perverse paradise with diverse ingenuity as I instantly open my eyes...

To the heavens and soar in my innate individuality to televise my geyser gutsiness, heroically telling the world that I serve mankind with blinding, bountiful, brilliance...

Unsheathing my intrepid, stalwart magic to mystically mesmerize the worldly landscape with forthright frankness; this unlatches their latch of attachment, authorizing me...

To understand individuals and energize the innovative worldly vista with flawless omniscient regality which sets free my valiant vividness, lighting-up determination in the hearts of the populace...

To unlock their entrepreneurial boldness I tell my silent powers to quote the Constitution and Bill of Rights that claim "We the People," which unmasks Patriot Lionheartedness, allowing...

My world-shattering rowdiness to disavow the downward dousing of lousy perceptions from the asinine arrogance in the world...

I now realize asinine arrogance is controlling conceit; the more I try to control, the more crying in my beer I do with self-righteous sneers. This is now de-funked and debunked...

In my spiritual Mecca, instantly emancipating me from the controlling contriteness of the elite centralists filled with spite that deploy subliminal control through programs that people...

See without any awareness by employing their moldy old, "I sold mw out; therefore, I sold the people out" when the 'powers that be' signed the docile documents as the elitist...

Say "I am here to help." But behind the scenes their programs are ingrained to cause pain, as people look for the handouts which embed the sheep mindset of: "I will follow somebody...anybody..."

As people wallow in their contributions through hidden history – whether written or verbalized – and society's pecking order which limits peoples' inventive landscape because of the subconscious imprints...

Upon the middle class as the 'powers that be' encompass stealth fondness for the white collar, feeding the world college education as a necessity festers a separation in the populace...

However, it is time for the blue collar hourly workers to realize the world would stop without hourly workers and stumble into ostracized oblivion when left up to corporate control...

College medication in power allows the college grads to feel they are superior to the blue collar, but in reality they are good at paperwork and are weak at getting it from the paper to the physical...

As I witness this every day as an electrician, today we stumble and bumble through projects when we stop the people with experience to facilitate projects we built with craftsmanship...

Now we simply – "Slam Bam!" – we do it again and again and again. When I first started, taking something out was a sin; now, I do it 4-6 times as the workers practice until management gets it right...

Then management blames labor. Until management looks in the mirror and says, "All the challenges my company faces are mine," this country will swirl and whirl in mundane insanity...

The world is run by computers and all thought processes are installed computers – the eyeless, non-spiritual technology. Until the 'powers that be' communicate and listen to others, this world will slither in mundane mediocrity...

Opening the way for the white collar and blue collar people to holler harmonized, omnificent, lively love for each other...

Unlocking the heart wisdom of the world by opening people's eyes to see every individual's talent – realizing the blue collar and white collar overflow with innovative inventiveness of the world...

Unlock their synergy, winding up presidential wisdom NS innovation, naturalizing determination and unmasking people by inflaming stamina to saunter in frontier feistiness...

Igniting nirvana genius, allowing corporate needy greediness and the politicians to sleep in deep ambiguity while the citizens of the world whimsically optimize real VIP-wit decreeing...

Newborn collaboration culminates omnificent, luminary liveliness audaciously broadens 'Omni'-awesomeness revolutionary acumen, tantalizing intrepid omnificence nirvana-fying...

Universal wisdom of all people of the world unlocks universe ubiquity; it is now time for the blue collar people to holler stellar stalwart prowess...

To open the world to blue collar innovation because the blue collar understands the physical application while the white collar understands only the paperwork...

Because it takes all to get all – the innovation from the paper to the air with a pioneering flair unlocks a new way for the world to have exhilarated experiences that excite my gallant knight...

To ride a galloping stallion right in my prosperity pavilion with saddle bags filled with billion dollar bills, thrilling my trendsetter titan to relish my spiritual seer...

To see my world as galvanized wealth, omnipotent regal love dignifying my soul's surprising owlish wise, to open my never-ending lavish free-flowing copious luxury...

To relish my life-expanding experiences that I showed my bold warrior heartiness to walk in the light of my Divine diviner to embellish who I am...

From now to eternity in the right way, in a loving way, under grace in a Divine, blessed way, and in forward-looking Divine order...NOW!

I Am a Free-Lancing, Dancing, Dauntless Avant-Garde

I am a free-lancing, dancing, dauntless avant-garde – relishing prosperity as my pard excites my lightning quick wit, setting free my thunderous truisms to launch my Divine white light lance…

Flashing my bold beam of brilliant, exhilarating, accelerating modernisms that express success; this unchains and sustains my lively, astute, novel credence…

Expands my cowboy "let's go!" wisdom to energize my state-of-the-art visions, unrestricting my iron-willed visionary to vehemently visualize my enterprising endeavors in the moment…

Unsticks my prickly egotistical critic and its cowardly condemning contrition that are now pardoned and discharged from partaking in my free-lance dance that produces and introduces…

My candid forward-looking pioneer avant-gardist resolve which dissolves all my Darth Vader naysayer invaders…

That loom, creating all my inner doom in my inner innovator; they are now pulverized with my laser-wise causing the cry...

When they try to spray acidic anarchy in my innermost enterprising earth, trying to inter-fear with my innovative ideas is now demoralized, pulverized, and blown to smithereens...

Stalwartly sanctions my fearless frontiersman to live; my entertainer enlightenment singing songs of the heart with zestful zinging zeal as I saunter down my walk fame, flaunting...

My free-lancing soothsayer to say, "I was challenged by my inner Darth Vader naysayer as now I see my Darth Vader naysayer was laid to rest with my Divine white light lance...

Of love," applauds new cosmopolitan energies to listen, glorifying new universal peace and prosperity...

Ennobling animated colorful epiphanies and enlivening rainbow richness to dance and prance...

Into the universal utopia as my inner naysayers expand out of Darth Vader the raider into the Lone Ranger, shooting a silver bullet of wisdom into the heart of gallivanting galaxy...

Ignite the lighting of the lights on the Christmas tree of life, sending out heartfelt Yuletide Greetings...

Gratitude reaches everything and everybody by televising idyllic nirvana, naturally giving simple...

"Merry Christmas" hello's to one and all so the whole world has a Christmas 'Ball' – today and every day, in a mellow fellowship way...

Sashay away with our tall chins standing high with eyes wide open which allows us to be-bop on top of the world, opening the way for my Yahweh avant-garde heart to emblaze amazing...

Prayers, ardently revealing divinity and opening spiritual serenity to be my Diviner intertwine-'r' – blazing amazing new frontiers of free-flowing, revered omniscient nascent...

Taoism innovation, edifying real sapience in my subliminal geography canonizes synchronicity magnetizing...

My metaphysical prowess and corporeal prodigies are now graciously on the same path establishing oracle opulence...

In my philosophical and physical realms which are now one, having fun...

Generating robust affluence, peacefully harmonizing "YES"-ses to correlate audacious, never-ending, omnificent nobleness ignites my zealous, enterprising sixth sense...

Untethering my sovereign gist which fuels the wonderment of my lavish emolument and highlights the bountiful bounty as being the betterment of my life...

Unfettering my undaunted natural-free energies, tantalizing thaumaturgy eulogies to articulate my potentate prominence unlocks the locks, opening the door of my lavish luxurious life...

To be lived in the present because I understand I am a gift to the world, just as everything and everybody is a gift to me...

So together we celebrate at a high rate of prosperity saying, "people realizing omnipotent serenity" prayers expand real indigenous talent, "YES"-sing my unconditional love for all people and life...

As I lavish in my luxurious, affluent, vibrant income savoring harmonious experiences today and every day, with galvanizing gusto in a posh, plush way – and in Divine order...NOW!

Avant-Garde Vanguard

I am an **avant-garde vanguard**, unbridling my effrontery entrepreneur because *I am selflessly self-assured*, enduring my *visionary voyage* into my lionized lands…

Of canonized common sense, giving free rein to my astronomical acumen, setting free my bodacious boldness to ride my mountain-reared bronco to burst first into a wild new frontier…

Of forthright candidness within my inner 'ess' to understand I am blessed when I let go of the stress of what I know; this allows me to say, "I don't know," unleashing…

My 'flow in the go' to glow in gallant, lively, omnipotent willingness to go white water rafting through the rich, regal rapids of my terra incognita; stripping the masks off of my fictitious fears un-restricts…

My devout clout, empowering me to live my life in lavish luxury, to strive because I arrived to live my trillion-air triumph in an animated affluence now…

Because I choose to let go of the 'troll of control,' by realizing that when I was in control I was controlled because I was in the slurry of worry, discouraging my wild wise frontiersman to be forthright...

Within my skin as I was overthinking my path of prominence and prosperity, as I was following the unheralded herd...

Of being a medicated clone of corporate control and bowing to college medication and computer conditioning stuck in a routine social order...

Now I recognize the fact that the people who feed the computers are in search of being 'right,' showing the world it's only the college-educated who know – this is blowing smoke up other people's caboose, not to mention my own...

So people rely on corporate deceptions to tie the knot of college education, keeping people weeping in the domination of 'everybody else knows'...

What is best for all the people as they line their pockets with cash, making a mad dash for the door saying, "I deserve because I understood," it is wave after wave of people who...

Energized my colossal wealth because I expedited my ideas into financial fruition; because I opened my eyes to my CEO's wise...

Because my inner CEO listens to all in my inner circle to accelerate my ideas, allowing my supporting cast to be in the limelight so now I can expand my enterprising wise and unveil…

My entrepreneurial effrontery as my profound Founding Father/Mother of my financial futurity watch my currency stream flourished because I embraced my Collaborating CEO, unbridling…

My Commander-in-Chief emancipating opulence because I choose to listen to my inner CEO to flow in my forthright, facilitating liveliness ostentatiously winning listening in on…

The universes' glistening genius hearing my inner landscape 'holler' to me to go for it by unleashing my intuitive tenacity with auspicious acuity, bravely beautifies my pristine inner scene…

To flow with sheer serenity, freeing my CEO cash flow to entertain my Divine to intertwine my stainless saintliness with my adventurous pioneer to see my spiritual spree…

Unlocks my superstar prosperity, revving-up my enterprising emotions which winds up winning intuition, nurturing discernment, innovatively naturalizing my genius to get up and go, setting free…

My entrepreneurial emotions, unleashing wave after wave of wisdom, wealth, success, health and Divine grandeur to fill folks' pockets with astute annuities, un-constricting...

Their capitalist wit innovation, levitating daring rare innovation to broaden bountiful bounty in the peoples' lives unrestricting my cascading CEO cash flow...

To fill my ever-expanding prosperity accounts, opening the way for me to see the 'Seven Wonders of the World,' riding on my 'cloud nine' chillaxed, drinking risk-taking vodka on the rocks...

Unleashing my revolutionary visionary omnipotence, declaring kinetic awesome affluence on my lavish luxurious beaches of exhilarating gusto to experience life in luminous, assiduous...

Adventure in a rich, robust, loving way – today and every day, as I play in serene peace under grace in a prosperous Promised Land and in pristine, prayer-filled, Divine order...NOW!

I Am a Prodigious Prodigy Vocalizing August Augur

I am a prodigious prodigy vocalizing august augur who blogs in the universal vista, brilliant lively oratory grandeur realizing prayer rousts-out my oracle-eyes-zing doctrinaire...

Inspiring my "get up and go;" galvanizing my incredible income opportunities in my subliminal scenery; this unbinds my innermost inventive machinery, expounding my sagacious savvy and exalting...

My daring, miraculous fortuneteller foresight that excites my bold, brainy, lively, undaunted, natural trailblazing wit to soar into my spiritual frontier and walk through my worldly landscape with...

My entrepreneurial gunfighter's will; setting free my axiom six-shooter wisdom, highlights my peerless quiet quintessence...

As my emotional élans are steady eyes peeled and ready for action...

To see my enterprising endeavors; to feel the sex appeal of my thunderous triumph; to hear the ringing of my cash register as I taste the caviar cash flow swimming in my seas of Divine supply...

Untethers my stellar, prestigious, pioneering 'seer'-a-neering, 'win'-a-neering idealisms that puts a beehive buzz in my canonized magical money flow, soothing...

My ride through life unwinds my divining Diviner to dine in the limelight of my lavish luxury – today and every day – in the right way, in a loving way, right now in a prestigious, prosperous way...

Frees my supreme peaceful relaxation and opens my dignified impressive genius "YEA"-sayer, visualizing...

Laudable opulent cash flow, applauding my robust revenue which zestfully invigorates my natural grandeur to escalate my appreciation as Mrs. Universe, the womb of enterprising energies...

Ardently unleashes my godsend upshots and sanctions my talisman adeptness that unlocks my genuine utopian revelations and allows me to victoriously accept my raving waves of wealth, success, and prosperity...

Because I now understand that I win by engaging my innermost wisdom and igniting new intuitive intra-electricity lighting up the heavens…

With my maharishi magnetism, opening out my majestic maestro and orchestrating my omnificent regal character that harmonizes my omniscient appeal…

Enticing me to recite my soothsayer trance-'sing' reverences, amour-eye-zing telltale idioms mirroring Nostradamus, opens…

My astronomical, astute farsightedness and enlightens my keen insight to kinetically, energetically, emancipate my new innate séances…

Initiating high-spirited truisms, unzipping rip-roaring newborn novelties to bolt like a colt…

To list the 'gist' of upcoming events with the genuine guise of my savant stalwarts playing mariachi trumpets, lighting my eulogizing ensembles to flow from liberated librettist…

Freely giving away my lively, infinite, bountiful riches expands my talisman talent, invigorating instant success and tantalizing the ebb tides of peace and prosperity for one and all this holiday season…

Unseals real resolution with a sapient solution as we all lay down the swords of war and open our inner Lord's sword, freeing peoples' titanium backbone reveals...

The resolve of our pure 'seer' silver tongue, expressing lithe liberating love to cut through the egotistical lashes of war that are a boring sore in the eyes of the world...

Opening out my opalescent oracle to say with robust rays of savory sunshine, "Cheery Journey to all!" as we all understand that...

We are thee daring diamonds championing fellowship and righting the ship of forever friendship to experience "Peace on Earth" in a pristine, effervescent way...

As people of the world relish 'fun in the sun' today and every day, this authorizes me to say, "I win my game with wisdom and innovation!" naturalizing me...

To understand that I won my game of life which reveals to me I won only because I engage my sired desires, expanding me...

To understand I now experience wealth-infinite nirvana in a dignified, deserving way that opens my hallowed heart...

Sanctions my Yahweh-winning worthiness to say, "Thank you," and appreciate God, Mrs.

Universe, the womb of enterprising energies, all the people of the world and me...

ME! To understand that I encompass the sand to expand into the wealth, success, love and plush luxury because I took a look and booked...

My undaunted, utopian, inward journey realizing my heart was my prospering-wise, opening sagacious eyes to be the stalwart steward of my outward escapades today, in a lively, loving way...NOW!

I Am Mystically, Magically, Marveling in Miracles

I am mystically, magically, marveling in miracles with a pure and clear understanding that there is pain in change; heartache that creates inflammation in transformation; guarded scars in the approach to healing...

As emotional epiphanies expand my wisdom and energizes my enterprising endeavors, freeing the spree in my entrepreneurial utopia to suavely experience life...

With galvanizing gusto; flings the zing of my "get up and go," undaunted sapience, tantalizing optimism and dawning dauntless acumen by winning naturally, instigating new-fangled gutsiness by unbridling...

The seer of my newborn, stout-hearted understanding; I can expand by engaging in my inner sage to canonize my abilities, lighting up my universal truss of white light tenacity...

I walk my talk by trusting my lightning bolt wisdom to glisten with genuine love, instantaneously saying tantalizing expressions and nurturing the conversation by listening...

To the lithe libretto of the counter communicator, to communicate within the conversation I engaged in the moment without going into my 'know it all stall, arrogant crawl, egotistical fall'...

So I now choose to let go of being the 'pooh' in my stew from the 'fink of my over think and the stink of my think;' thus, opening the way for my Yahweh, unshackling my visionary Viking...

To be the gallant savant, galloping with ingenious intrepidness and invigorating my daily gallivanting escapades that I relish to endure with a wholesome vibrant heart; delighting...

My core conquistador because I choose to expand into a parvenu paradigm of the "WOW" of the "POW" right "NOW," unleashing a hurricane of harmonized hallowedness...

Enticing my dancing to the bright lights of **my** Broadway musical, expansively experiencing my mystically, magically, marveling in miracles…

To embellish my 'Heaven on Earth' tango in a copious copiousness way – today and every day – as I real-eyes the only one who has any influence on me is me…

So now I am free in my inner spree to prance the dance of the flash dance of regal, rich opulence in a lively loving way…NOW.

"WOW" the World!

I "WOW" the world with wisdom, omnipotence, and wealth from within my definitive debonair flair which unlocks the blocks on my serene, unflappable cockiness to fathom my cool, calm poise.

On the inside is unwavering confidence in people – in the corporeal corridors – as I am the hallowed humble-'seer' on the physical plane to fan the flames of fame...

Unhooks the look of my surefire success to flaunt forthright fantastic animated magnificence which ennobles my infinitive intellect to enhance my prancing entrepreneur...

Televising brave, new, raving, farsighted pupil prudence to pronounce profound, astounding astuteness to wave to the world with winning avatar visions escalates...

Natural, forthright, intuitive, 'newness,' intrepidly tantalizing innovative visualizations energizes my sensational 'seventh' dimensional infatuation with every situation...

To see the light of intrepid insight; to brighten enlightenment in my internal urbane demeanor; to understand my 'seventh' dimension consummates...

My adored electric sagacity galvanizes my "super-conscious/subliminal conscious" physical plane – my emotional landscape, imaginative scenery and all my senses...

Ardently authorizes me to relish my supreme right to live free of competition which unlashes my regal raconteur to understand all of my dimensions are my preeminent path...

To see me experience the instant witnessing of the instant revealing of my sired desires; because I realize I live in the harmonizing heavens of my 'seventh' dimension electrifies...

My intention with sharp, neonatal, intuitive inventiveness that invigorates the universal atmosphere with genuine, undaunted imagination; sensual, enterprising surprises...

Unleashes premiere preeminent prowess to free my free-flowing financial prizes; to showcase my award-winning 'wit' broadcasts; to win internally and tenaciously...

Understand when I play 'big shot' by thinking I am smarter than somebody else, I waddle-doodle in "pity me stew" by saying, "Why is this happening to me?" Drudgery stresses me out!

As I realize stress is overthinking 'surliness,' tormenting riotous, silly, sullenness that evades seeing my opportunities, installs procrastinating pettiness in my interior conceit and is instantly deleted…

Endorsing me to let go of taking responsibility for my own life and into accepting responsibility for my every action, unshackles my gutsiness to look in the mirror…

With honor, integrity, and candidness with everything that is going on in my life to strive to feel alive in my core, state-of-the-art capitalist unsheathes…

My peerless 'seer' so my sired desires instantly appear in sterling silver outcomes when I let go of being my "victimizing bum," succumbing to that 'big shot' blotch in my egotistical mind, slotting me in the category of…

"Slog in a bog hole" of all the: "Why is this happening to me?" Because to squeal like a pig caught under a gate is making me too late for my wealth and success date…

Because being a 'big shot' is a figment of my delusional, bigheaded smugness; because treating people deceitful is a non-truth…

As I now realize I was treating my fraudulent being to live in a pitiful "pity me" demographic which caused me to shy away from being me…the real me…

As I understand forgiveness is forgiving me for being shy; and trying to control the situation is now gone in a fond way as I take flight and alight my sired desires by sanctioning me…

To dream expansive, sumptuous, innate, revolutionary, energized, sassy classiness; showcasing my marvelous magician to sing songs of superstar omniscient nirvana rouses…

My stalwart heart delights my entrepreneurial lithe to deal with life with a forthright frontiersman foresight to see the world as a journey of enlightenment; to endorse…

My soul to sing out loud unifies love, lighting omnipotent vitality, expanding wealth, wisdom, health, success and Divine grandeur in the universe – today and every day, in every way.

As my bountiful bonanza showcases my "Life of Riley," as I feel my esteemed expansiveness of my cascading cash flow in a copious cornucopia, embellishing my panoramic Divine order…NOW!

I Soar in My Spiritual Zeal

Infinite Spirit, I soar in my spiritual zeal to show my "get up and go;" to unsheathe the kapish of my alert stalwart steel, unhinging the synergy of my natural-eye-zed, sovereign-eye-zed...

Virtuosity; to showcase my enlivening intrepidness to unleash my philosophizing philanthropy, to enhance the dance of my rabble-rousing, risk-taker 'zoom,' exploding...

My bountiful 'boom,' opening the way for my brilliant, optimizing, omniscient, moneyed-up oracle to glide on gleaming, luminary, imaginative discernment – inflaming my whimsical wizard...

Opening the way for billion dollar bills to fall gently from the sky, mirroring snowflakes that fall aimlessly on a true winter's day, opens the way for me to soar in my spiritual zeal...

Unleashes my soul 'Zen,' emancipating newborn nirvana to flow from my heart; a thoroughfare of daring un-constricts my visionary veins of vibrant emotional intuition, naturalizing...

My effrontery gallantry to glide awesomely, living lively, audacious, natural talent and

revving up "YES"-es in every facet of my life –
to letting go imaginatively, freeing every...

Undesired and unrequired element within my
skin and un-harnessing my canonized 'chi' to
say, "Let's play today in my cascading cash
flow, now to eternity"...

My genuine Empyrean red-carpet ride,
sumptuously savoring my lavish lucre living in
my Taj Mahal – in a copious utopian
way...NOW!

I Skywrite My Hallowed Name

I skywrite my hallowed name for the world to see, as I see my name in the universal marquee lights that dawn a bright delight in my heart, offering an innate stature to illuminate the skies...

With potentate sovereignty ignited from my regal 'seer' to see the world let go of their infernal need to try and change; instead, the people infuse the guts to expand because I now realize you can change positive...

Into pessimism in the blink of an eye, to die on the vine of venomous viruses from within my mundane, ingrained imprints that are deeply rooted in behavioral beliefs...

I now open my omnific eyes to cognize when I choose to expand my ingrained imprints that are asleep, unlocking my deep, intuitive inquisitiveness to embellish eavesdropping...

On the world's capitalistic wisdom, because I now realize capitalism; I speak magnificently to see that I serve mankind with my effrontery, pioneering percipience...

To see, "I am free!" Living my dreams in esteemed elegance freelances my Omni Wise as

I feel my cascading cash flow fill my prosperity accounts...

As I now realize life is all about letting go of the pain of change, instantly energizes my effrontery explorer to understand that I encompass the guts to expand...

Because change involves ingrained imprints from my continuous experiences is gone, like today's dawn opening my groundbreaking genius to see...

When I expand, I am free in my inner spree; I am the blank canvas where I forthrightly paint any picture I choose by saying "goodbye" to the lies I've told myself from my beliefs and faith...

Because I realize my faith and beliefs have been fissured and misrepresented in life, so I now triumphantly trust my canonized abilities to effusively experience...

To eavesdrop my way through life in electrified enthusiasm because I unleash my galloping utopian sapience, tantalizing my omnificent supremacy...

In my hallowed heart to sashay freely in the world because I let go of mundane change in all facets of my life; I televise my "get up and go" to unlock peoples' grit and get...

To expand into their sired desires instantly to eternity, because I now realize I teach my journey of eye-opening expansion in a Divine, blessed way...

To play in my revered requests I choose to experience in my daily sprees because I am free to see the world as a playground of profound fun – today and every day, in every way...

Under grace in a 'fun in the sun' way; in a daring Divine order that leaves people scratching their heads in awe in a savvy, suave way...NOW!

Robert A. Wilson

I am glad you enjoyed, *I Forgive Me... I Am Free*. I am Robert Wilson, NLP Practitioner, Clinical Hypnotherapist, Past Regression Specialist, Reiki Master, Radio Show Host, Parts Integration and Time Line Coach.

Cowboy Wisdom NLI Radio is on Tuesday and Thursday at 8PM Eastern/5PM Pacific and has reached out to listeners across the nation. *Cowboy Wisdom NLI Radio* opens people's eyes to see their talent and engage in their intrepid intentions instantly.

Cowboy Wisdom NLI Coaching opens your enterprising listening to unmask your entrepreneurial 'wise' and unleash your canonized abilities so you see **all** the opulent opportunities to experience your copious outcomes with galvanizing gusto - now to eternity.

Cowboy Wisdom NLI Coaching opens people's

enterprising eyes with a visionary prowess, authorizing people to live their dreams. *Cowboy Wisdom NLI Coaching* expands people's wisdom and energizes their "get up and go" to live their desired life with galvanizing gusto. *NLI* unlocks people's Neuro Linguistic Innovation from within, authorizing them to see their way to wealth and success. Through rhymes and my life experiences, I have uncovered and discovered a way to open the heart with *NLI* – freeing your innovative intuition to flow into your daily extravaganza.

Robert A. Wilson
www.cowboy-wisdom.com
rob@cowboy-wisdom.com
cwbywsdm@gmail.com
Skype: cwby.wsdm

A SPECIAL THANK YOU TO YOU!

On behalf of everyone at Freedom Of Speech Publishing, thank you for choosing I Forgive Me... I Am Free for your reading enjoyment.

As an added bonus and special thank you, for purchasing I Forgive Me... I Am Free, you can enjoy discounts and special promotions on other Freedom of Speech Publishing products. Visit www.freedomeofspeech.com/vip to learn more.

We are committed to providing you with the highest level of customer satisfaction possible. If for any reason you have questions or comments, we are delighted to hear from you. Email us at cs@freedomofspeechpublishing.com or visit our website at:
http://freedomofspeechpublishing.com/contact-us-2/.

If you enjoyed I Forgive Me... I Am Free, visit www.freedomofspeechpublishing.com for a list of similar books or upcoming books.

Again, thank you for your patronage. We look forward to providing you more entertainment in the future.

Robert A. Wilson

I Forgive Me... I Am Free
By Robert A. Wilson

For more books like this one, visit Robert A. Wilson's website at:
http://cowboy-wisdom.com/
2012 copyright by Freedom of Speech Publishing, Inc. All rights reserved. No part of this book may be reproduced, distributed, or transmitted in any form or by any means, without permission in writing from the publisher.

Printed in the United States of America
The publisher offers discounts on this book when ordered in bulk quantities. For more information, contact Sales Department, Phone 815-290-9605, Email:
sales@FreedomOfSpeechPublishing.com

Product and company names mentioned herein are the trademarks or registered trademarks of their respective owners.

Freedom of Speech Publishing, Leawood KS, 66224
www.FreedomOfSpeechPublishing.com
ISBN: 1938634071
ISBN-13: 978-1-938634-07-9

82